ANCHOR
BOOKS

POSITIVE THOUGHTS

Edited by

Heather Killingray

First published in Great Britain in 1998 by
ANCHOR BOOKS
1-2 Wainman Road, Woodston,
Peterborough, PE2 7BU
Telephone (01733) 230761

HB ISBN 1 85930 686 1
SB ISBN 1 85930 681 0

FOREWORD

Anchor Books is a small press, established in 1992, with the aim of promoting readable poetry to as wide an audience as possible.

We hope to establish an outlet for writers of poetry who may have struggled to see their work in print.

The poems presented here have been selected from many entries. Editing proved to be a difficult task and as the Editor, the final selection was mine.

We all have a hidden gift within us which allows us to express ourselves in our own special ways.

The poems in this collection are a result of that gift and for the poets included in this anthology it is a unique way of unveiling matters close to their hearts, amusing tales or stories about people they either love, hate or envy.

A variety of poems ranging in style and length are brought together to create a superb book full of the laughter and mirth of life.

I trust this selection will delight and please the authors and all those who enjoy reading poetry.

Heather Killingray
Editor

CONTENTS

THANKS AND APOLOGIES

For all the times, that you held me,
To comfort me, when I cried,
For all the times, when the 'monsters' were prowling,
And you stayed by my side,
For all the days and the nights spent in vigil,
Praying, when I was unwell,
For the countless times that you helped me,
Far too numerous, to tell,
For your wisdom, your guidance and knowledge,
You gave to me throughout the years,
For your love, your kindness and friendship,
And for every one of your tears,

I thank you

For all of the times that I hurt you,
And caused you in anguish to cry,
For the times that the truth was demanded,
But instead, I told you a lie,
For the nights that you spent in torment,
When I was nowhere to be seen,
And the times in stubborn defiance,
I told not, where I had been,
For all the worry, the fretting and heartache,
I have caused you throughout the years,
And for every one of your heartfelt,
Salty, falling tears.

I apologise

R S Strong

SWEET DREAMS

I thought I heard a noise last night while lying in my bed,
The sweetest voice you've ever heard and this is what it said
'Your life is yours to keep and in each direction you will learn
But, sometimes you will feel all alone and won't know where to turn'

I asked what should I do when I am feeling low,
The voice said 'Don't worry your heart will show you where to go'
I said 'It feels too hard sometimes when there's
                                        many decisions to make'
Then it said 'I promise you when you're weak I'll show you the
                                        road to take'

I was troubled by such a promise, one so hard to keep
It heard my thoughts so clearly, saying 'Shush my child and sleep'

While drifting in and out of dreams I asked the voice its name
'You know my name' he said, 'You called and so I came'
Once more I was puzzled, no name had I said
He said you did remember as you knelt against your bed

All of a sudden a bright light commenced from the heavens above
The Lord had come to visit me and guide me with his love.

Lisa Jane Khan

A NURSERY GARDEN

Springtime magic everywhere, the trees they are no longer bare.
Blossom fragrant pink and white sparkling in the morning light.
Petals falling through the leaves like confetti in the breeze.
A little girl wanders there with pretty dress and dark brown hair.
She's sat beneath a cherry tree, her dress in folds across her knee.
She looks so pretty sitting there pink blossom falling in her hair.
Small hands reach up for her to catch, the fragile petals in her lap.
A child's first experience of wondrous things.
The beauty of spring's awakening.

Shirley Holt

PLEASE LET US

Let the heavens open up and rain down love
Let our spirits rise high above and soar like a dove
Let a gentle peace touch every soul and heart
Let us all feel hope and make a brand new start
Let us all live in happy unison, no more war and pain
Let us put our arms aside so no more blood will stain
Let our tongues be still and use no words to judge
Let everyone forgive and no longer hold a grudge
Let us all try and live together side by side
Let a new society emerge that will have pride.

Marlene Mullen

YOUR ETERNAL FLAME

Your eternal flame burns deeply in my soul,
To You I call, you make me whole.
Without your kindly loving care
I despair.

The promise that You made to me
Is in Your book where all can see.
A torch that lights to give the way
As I peruse it every day.

This blaze that warms my heart so strong
Leads me to righteousness and away from wrong.
I bathe in the reflective glory
And read the unfolding story.

A story of God and His Son most high
The developing theme makes me cry,
These tears pierce the eternal flame
As I remember Your ceaseless name.

Denise Shaw

TIME JUST DRIFTS AWAY

The dawn rises far above me,
The breeze blows through my hair.
I walk the sandy shoreline,
In love without a care.
I feel the ocean ripples,
As I walk each step to him.
My heart is beating faster,
My breath is held within.
As I move up close beside him,
His eyes look down to say,
Do you feel the way that I do,
Do hunger night and day,
Is the yearning in you strong enough?
If it is I beg you stay.
I softly place a fingertip
Ssshhh! No more said this day.
I embrace his soul and love him
And let time just drift away
The feeling of the waves wash over me
From the ocean's bed of love
I surrender to his tenderness
I'm locked within his love.

Rhonda K Russell

THE MAKER OF BRIDGES

Ah! There you are,
I have searched these fields for you near and far.
Little girl it is time to go,
Your people await or don't you know.

They became worried when you didn't appear,
Through the gates much to their fear.
These meadows are vast and forever endless,
Where the spirit doth walk when the mind becomes senseless.

It's time to arise and to take my hand,
And to walk the path of shadows towards God's promised land.
Over the hill where the sun shines bright,
To the heart of thy clan and to what is right.

Pass through those gates, your kith are yonder,
It is time for me to go back unto my wander.
Lest I forget, the babes are no longer,
Their early release made six adults the stronger.

Time to grieve, by prayer and by song,
A dynasty created, their matriarch now gone.
Many a tear as yet to be shed,
For that little old lady who now lies dead.

There you are son, it's time to go,
Time for you to stop crying or didn't you know.
Take my hand, I'll take you home,
These fields are but dreams and of no place to roam.

D B Allan

THE LOST CAT RETURNS FROM THE COLD

The wintry morning sun reveals the Old Cat scratching at the door,
His cries are heard, he enters and creeps across the floor.
Straight to his bowl of food he plunges in as if he had never
tasted food before.

Where has he been, what has he done?
A prodigal's return at the rising of the sun.
The cold nights away from home, for him were they any fun?

Maybe he found a sheltered place,
A warm hearth-side, a friendly face,
Or did he hide shivering in fear and cold from the dangers that
afflict his feline race?

But he is home now in warmth and loving care,
As he sleeps in his favourite place will his thoughts with us
he will share?
Maybe now he is home in safety, he does not have a care.

David J Gaywood

AN APPLE FALLS

You can't tell an apple when to fall,
Or the sea to turn the tide,
You can't tell a bird to sing,
Or a groom to wed a bride.

You can't stop a river rippling,
Or the moon to shed its light,
Nor stop the sun from shining,
Or change the day to night.

But you can make folks happy,
And help the passers-by,
And to help your neighbours,
Without asking the reason why.

Then thank the Lord for living,
And place your hand in prayer,
And love all God's creatures,
And show them that you care.

Nancy Scott

DO YOU KNOW?

If you were to look at me
With a question in your eyes,
Would you see,
What I know?

If you were to offer your arms,
And enfold me in a warm embrace,
Would you hear,
What I know?

If you were to let me rest,
In tender silence upon your chest,
Would you understand,
What I know?

If you were to begin that kiss,
Expressing soft expectant hope,
Would you feel,
What I know?

If you were to ask the question,
With love and patience and hesitation,
You would speak,
What I know.

Pauline Nash

MY SON

It is so, my son has taught me from heaven above,
While I watched him go.
That true happiness comes from love

Though in great pain he showed his love
The sorrow I felt I must not show,
It is so, my son has taught me from heaven above

He lay still as though in a pool of mud,
He knew it was true though he felt so low
That true happiness comes from love.

Death came swift like the wings of a dove,
His body wasted, my love for him did stronger grow,
It is so, my son has taught me from heaven above.

His bed was placed in an alcove above,
Watching it I felt so low, but knowing it was so,
That true happiness comes from love.

In uniforms that fitted like a glove,
The nurses watched with deep sorrow,
It is so, my son has taught me from heaven above,
That true happiness comes from love.

A R Kemp

DANCING A DREAM

In a dreamer's life
we act out our dreams
until we reach perfection,
in a dreamer's life
of passion and lust.

I've tried to avoid deception

And today there's no exception.

Like the passion of a rose
my life is now so perfect
in my love I find no flaw,
pure desire and emotions
with my heart at heaven's door,
as I feel my affections
in the midnight rain
I know her love is there
through good times and bad
and times when love ain't fair,
And as I dance the dream
from this day on
I know what road to take
as I follow the feelings that unbound my heart
the dreams of life I make . . .

and now I know I'm dancing a dream.

I P Smyth

THE MAY-NOT QUEEN

If you wake, don't call me early,
leave me sleeping Mother dear;
Tomorrow'll be the rottenest time
of all the sad new year;
Of all the sad new year, mother
the lousiest, horriblest day
'Cos I'll not be Queen o' the May Mother,
I'll not be Queen o' the May.

There's many a black, black eye, Mother,
But none so black as mine;
I got in a fight last night, Mother,
He hit me too hard, the swine.
I've put a piece of steak on it,
(this butchering game's a racket)
I had to purloin a nice bit of sirloin
and Mum, it did cost me a packet!

But rain or shine tomorrow,
I'm going to the fair.
I'll gaze upon the throne of the May
Queen,
and wish that I sat there.
If fine I'll take my parasol,
if wet, my big umbrella,
But I'll never be Queen o' the May because,
let's face it Mum, I'm a fella!

John Harrison

MERLIN'S DREAM

The rising sun was having fun with the misty morning dew,
Carmarthen Town was feeling down hung over from a few.
The schooner frail was setting sail for countries wide and far,
And the girls all sang 'penillion' outside the Jolly Tar.

Well, Merlin's Hill was standing still above the Towy sound,
He cast his wand on Bishop's Pond and magic shone around.
The river flowed beside the road down to the sandy bar,
And the girls all sang 'penillion' outside the Jolly Tar.

Well, pots and pails and old wives' tales and legends long forgot,
Goodwill and cheer and poor man's beer frequent the Coffee Pot.

He sold his ware in the market square to feed his family fair,
He sold his charms in the Tanner's Arms without a second care.
The wine was good and the men all would forget the new found star,
But the girls all sang 'penillion' outside the Jolly Tar.

Well, fleece and geese and twelve police and coracles on the quay,
The tide was wide by the riverside beneath the arches three.

Well, the ships no more caress the shore or kiss the harbour way,
But Merlin's well and his magic spell adorns the precinct grey.
The salmon pools and the grammar schools have long declined afar,
But the girls still sing 'penillion' outside the Jolly Tar.

Clive Jones

JOY

What is a poem or prose
Some deep emotions in your soul
It's tempestuous feelings that must come out
To tell the world to sing and shout
To show your joy and even pain
To know how much we'll gain
By feeling all these lovely things
Your heart will surely find its wings.

Mary Tickle

THE CHRISTMAS VISITOR

The air is still - the night is cold
Some shelter I must find
So I creep to a stall where a baby lies
The saviour of all mankind
Mary his mother is oh so proud
For she has given birth
To the son of God - the Holy child
God's greatest gift to earth
The skies aglow - the stars are bright
And glory shines around
While I am in my lowly place
Just scuttling on the ground
He can hear the cattle gently low
And know that they are there
But I've no voice - so may he hear
My silent thankful prayer
The shepherds come to worship him
To where the star has shone
But I must scurry out of sight
Lest I get trod upon
The wise men come, and they can place
Their gifts before his cot
But I have nothing I can give
Save all the love I've got
Yet - though they come with gold and myrrh
This infant child to meet
I can crawl where no one sees
To worship at his feet
And I can rest on the very spot
His precious head does lay
So I thank God that I am just
A spider in the hay.

Irene Beattie

TERRORISTS

They cannot be brothers, sisters or lovers,
With mirrored reflections of shame.
No God, no religion, even rats have precision,
The will for decision,
A name!

Puppets who dance to the piper's tune,
Paying with souls whilst their masters croon.
Puppets who pay for their leader's sin,
Stripped of the right to be human within!

Pity for those with blood on hand . . .
Pity for the beautiful land . . .
Pity for the country's folk,
For united peace many have spoke.

Pity for Ireland's future child
If Ireland cannot be reconciled;
For a future ruled by the IRA
The green will turn to red one day.

Doreen Welby

ANGEL ABSOLUTE

Bury me when I die, I want to fade to soil,
In a graveyard with an atmosphere like no other place at all,
A place of hush, peace, grace.
Rows and rows of headstones standing the test of time,
Some cracking and crumbling with age.
Each symbol of loss, covered in moss, hiding poetic page,
Words to stir emotions, that get stronger for the younger,
And the people they left behind.
We'll all be history one day, be forever beneath the ground,
With our names and ages written in stone,
There seems nothing so profound.
Life should be taken by the hand, lived to the brim each day,
Worry not, hurry not, nothing happened can be changed.

When I lie in my eternal bed, don't stand over me and weep,
Stand and smile, remember our times, memories are for keeps.

Claire Glover

MY TREASURE ISLAND

I found a place of solitude,
On an island by the sea,
In a desolate location,
That's what appealed to me.

Sheltered by the cliff-tops,
Tucked back inside a bay,
Stormy seas and howling winds,
Called to me night and day.

I roamed the rocky hillsides,
With glowing cheeks so red,
Many mixed emotions,
Unwinding in my head.

I laughed, I cried and spoke out loud,
To the only friend I had,
Treasuring all good memories,
Rebuking all the bad.

The time had come for me to leave,
God was kind with me,
He gave me peace, a chance to dwell,
And then He set me free.

Christine Shannon

MY MUM

My mum is so great
She does everything for me
She irons my dresses
And cooks my tea.

My mum is the best
The best one you've seen
She tidies my room
And does a great job for me.

My mum is so cool
She never is dull
I'm glad I've got her
Because she's the number one!

Kirsty Corbett (11)

ASPIRATIONS OF AN ORPHAN

A frog in my throat sings with glorious wet contentment; splashing itself with brown liquid as I raise my Guinness glass with foaming white head to my lips on Brighton beach.

In my memory there is someone crying pebble-shaped tears on a pebble beach - crying for human comfort and warmth. She is without mother, father or friend. She longs for self-proclaim - action, recognition, worldly success and roaring notorious embraces.

She is as wild as the wind-blown scorched sand. Wild as the leaping waves breaking down her dreams. She yearns for appreciation of her life's pattern as the waves recede under the light of the orange-glowing sunset from her paddling feet. Her pattern of wanting to be wanted - to be included in God's world embracing vital love fill her with yearning.

Her emotions are as brittle as dry bones. She feels she is just flotsam or jetsam on the bench of life. She belongs to no-one. In the midst of a crowded beach she feels herself an isolated castaway.

In her bones she aches for free expression for the love and joy she feels. Her held-in child's voice, her held-in tears, held-in laughter and held-in desire to dance, sing leap and rejoice with a reciprocating companion, overwhelms her. The packed down repression of her life is winding up to an explosive force, her body tenses as it awaits the trigger to set off a mighty blast.

Her held-in life when she was not allowed to lose control, not allowed to dissolve into choice or to reorientate herself into her own pattern of becoming had plagued her youth. She longs for the beautiful soul that will burst within her and set her free from inhibition.

She longs for her own maturity to become one with women of depth, of warmth and glorious wide vision. To be sparked with a firework mind within a vibrant free body. To become a welcome member of the band of singing, laughing, vital life.

Ruth Kitzinger

THE NEIGHBOUR

I wish I'd taken time to say
'Good morning, what a lovely day'
And talk about the news and weather
Passed the time of day together.
But I'd pass you by without a thought
Excuse myself of any fault
For I lived such a hectic life
As mother, daughter, house-maid, wife
The memories that you tried to share
Took far more time than I could spare
I knew you lived there on your own
And faced the endless days alone
Between my house and yours next door
It must have seemed a mile or more
I've heard they found you on the floor
You'd been there since the day before
Belatedly I think of ways
I might have cheered your lonely days
How I wish I'd paused to say
'Good morning, what a lovely day.'

Janet Brown

BEAUTY AND THE SNOB

Smart clean jeans
New and tight
Designer sweat
Logo top right.

Neat . . . discreet.

Natural beauty
She is aware
Preening windowed reflection
Fluffing hair.

A mobile phone
Her fashion must
Will it work
Can she trust?

Jingle tones announce a call
Self importance
Standing tall.

'Allo mate, yeah course it's me, zat yu?
Want tu meet?'

West London patois disappoints this snob
My hypocrisy trespass now complete.

D I Ross

BUT!

Some say they don't hear tradesmen whistling any more,
But, I do! Skylarks in short supply? But, I hear them too!
That Christmas is a racket, yes, it is . . . but pause, reflect . . .
God's still in the 'Biz'!
That there is far more 'push and shove' (I agree!) -
But, Christ still comes to fill our hearts with love.
'But he's not relevant,' I hear some cry.
But - I say, 'For you He came to live and die.'
But you may know *He* is not dead at all,
(Adam and Eve knew Him well before their fall!)
I've put these 'buts' before you on this day,
And trust by reading them you find the Way!

Patricia Lawrence

RESPONSE TO WILLIAM SHAKESPEARE

'Tis true! - The world's a stage,
And all the people on it are but players!
With one long drama only to unfold,
No practice runs - no matinees - but only
One unrehearsed performance, through the scenes
In all the stages that each life involves!
But 'no man is an island' and our
Lives will, and do, impinge on others too!
In fact, so many things impinge on our performance,
Distractions, hold-ups, accidents, emotions - just a few!

So few can give an Oscar-winning show!
For most of us the effort proves too much;
But as the proverb says 'hope springs eternal'
And so, we struggle on from stage to stage - expecting
The next one to be better than the last.
I've reached the final stage of my performance
The others all behind me, and I'm tiring,
Now, as I go through each day I'm ever thinking
Of all the 'yesterdays' I've seen so far!
Yes, there were happy days, and there were sad,
And sometimes too, along the way, I reckon things were bad!
But now my glances are all backward cast
As shadows from the past fall on my path!
And looking now I reckon I can see,
I tried to make a difference - that was me!
It hasn't all been easy, I confess
But I taught the kids that one should do their best,
For people all around them, and give help
To those who need it as they journey on.
My part in life's great drama is unsung.
I've never conquered Everest - nor won,
World Cups, Olympic Gold, Nobel Prizes or such like,
I simply played my part - the very best I could,
And more than that - I simply could not give!

Elizabeth Tumilty

THE SEVEN STAGES

Entrance, twins are born, mother holds each one with tenderness
Both parents celebrate the good news with great happiness
How can they tell them apart, for both twins are identical
One has brown eyes the other blue, enters five minutes early that's all,

Second stage, when small children, the twin with brown eyes
is taken away
Where angels sing in heaven, under God's loving care to stay
A beautiful place, where there is no pain or suffering
The twin that is left behind, is far too young for the understanding

Third stage, school should be the best days, but sometimes her
a failer,
As time goes by soon time to leave, but not much learning, does
no favour
When a teenager high hopes are there, for the future ahead
No clock can be turned back, there may be regrets instead

Through womanhood, lovers meet to steal the very first kiss
Just like a midsummer's night dream, and such lovely bliss
But, when love departs, sorrow may take part, stage four
If fate is kind again, love will find its way back, I am sure

Stage five, marriage takes place, golden rings are exchanged
When they are joined together, preparations are then arranged
Through time, children arrive, joy is again shared together
Until, their youthful years are reached, even through the departure

Once, wearing long dresses, high heel shoes, the woman is left
somehow
When that love passes by, fate again has its way anyhow
When sorrow falls or destiny fails, just seek God above, stage six
For God makes all things possible, for everything that exists

From generation to generation that makes the world go round
Search for peace as a new century enters, and love will be found
Exits the six stages, through this past strange history
Seventh stage, remember God is the beginning, and finish, and will be
through each century

Jean P McGovern

DEATH'S ANGELS

the room came alight with the glow of your smile
a heart so pure as white as the snow that night
and when the time came for you to go
thy mighty spirit called the strong and the weak,
the near and the far - seven elders to herald thy way

vigil at thy side . . .

a sigh from many days of silence
as you bade your last goodbye
from a deep sleep two gentle teardrops cried
the love inside the day you died
bathed in the final veiled water, blessed by the prayer

hosts of angels gathered around waiting that solitary moment
as thy path was cleared without a sound
thy sacred soul to bear safe to heaven in glory crowned

silence in four corners . . .

silent strength brushed thy cheek in comfort;
silent guardian watched o'er in reverence;
silent head bowed in veiled prayer in faith;
as silent helper cleared the way;

silent victory, a silent battle won,
silence as the angels bore thy soul away

white candle at dawn in solitude, bathed in tranquil prayer
angel musk scented the air, lingering on from nowhere

crystals turned their faces as angels bore you high
heavenly scents flowed as the carriage passed by
white lilies bathed ivy, as the ivy in your name
realmed high in deep purple iris, as a diamond array
clothed in flowing satin and lace for that final day

advent harked the herald angels that sung
farewell choirs as morning broke with heaven's life begun

... yea the truth seen

Lynne T Stuart

UNTITLED

From whenst all came,
I doth not know the truth,
In the light and of that the rain,
From whenst all came,

Above and beyond the call of time,
From whenst all came,
For it is only I that can take the blame,
From whenst all came,

All of things that there may be,
All of things that might have been,
The goodness of within,
From whenst all came,

It is I shall show forth thy right,
And purify thy mind,
And deepen that soften heart,
From whenst all came,

'Tis you that is in need to look,
Above the call and beyond,
In the stillness of time,
From whenst all cometh.

Jessica Wright

THE HUMAN RACE

What a disgrace is your human race
As you pull each brother down,
The colour of your skin
Seems to be a sin
For the black, white, yellow or brown.

You've lost the savvy to mediate,
You just sleaze each other's name,
And with all your good intentions
Inflict bitterness, hate and shame.

You criticise then compromise,
Twist meanings causing pain.
You're simply stupid idiots
Who just haven't got a brain.

Your fighting is so meaningless
You insult that same old story,
By trying to call it freedom
It's just power, and the glory.

Your sands of time are running out
The world's coming to an end,
Soon you will be all alone
With nothing to defend.

So heed this simple message
Before you are all gone!
Reconcile and love your brother
And for 'Christ's' sake please be one.

Les Campbell

ALL MANKIND WERE BORN NO ANGEL

All mankind were born no angel,
And felt only the warmth of a mother's breast
For his first comfort. Soon thoughts began
To multiply; and his first view
Upon this new world seemed deep and wide,
Gathering toys and excitement. Then flowers
Of youth, the snotty-nosed schoolboy,
Weighted down with books and a prayer
To feed his mind and soul; measles and cough
Syrup fed his ills. Then the young man,
Full of self confidence and fashion dressed
To aim Cupid's bow and arrow straight
At the heart of his chosen, to take and hold
Till death do part. Then the greatest advent,
The family man, the provider,
The street-wise community chess player.
And then reading spectacles and grey hair
Thinning like Robin, sorrow meet sorrow,
His elders die, and the will of life
Is giving birth to the joy of being
A balding grandfather. Eft the autumn breeze
Of life, the second coming of childhood,
With a slight stoop and his walking stick,
Aching bones wish that they could run
Like they used to run, and even to begin
All life again. Lastly, a fragile
And thin figure, still with memory of life,
Opened and closed his eyes, content.
Save genes, save DNA, then save the soul.

Robin Pearcey

A CHILD OF WAR

The child's body lay on the ground a shallow empty shell,
The nightmare over a release from this living hell,
His days filled with guns, bombs and war,
No parents to love him no-one to adore,
He'd lost them long ago, left alone to survive,
Killing others, doing anything he has to, to stay alive,
The days and nights were dark for him every day,
No chance to make friends, go out and play,
He's now gone to a place where others have gone before,
At last he'll be welcomed through an open door,
He'll find peace as God lays his hand upon his head,
He's at rest, no more worries now he's dead.
Gone now to a far better place,
Frown lines, sadness and tears disappear from his face,
Ours is not to reason why, young innocent children die,
He'll be laid to rest in an unmarked grave,
His life we were unable to save,
But this child's life was not in vain,
If in the future from wars we do abstain.

Trudy Lapinskis

THE LADY REFLECTS

When I was sixteen
I was pristine.

When I was twenty
Getting plenty.

When I was thirty
Still quite flirty.

When I was forty
Haughty and naughty.

When I was fifty
Pretty nifty.

When I was sixty
Eyes were misty.

Now I am seventy.
Well, I can dream, can't I?

Frank Henry

GENERATIONS

My grandmother was the sort of granny that you might meet in a book -
Plump and smiling and comfortable and such a very good cook.
With her snowy white hair and her black velvet dress
She always was ready to greet and to bless.
With a bowl and a spoon she could mix and bake
A wonderful, buttery rich fruit cake.
To shop on a Sunday to her was a sin,
So was picking up cards, or a needle or pin.
We called her old-fashioned, and she'd quietly say
'Well, I like to do things in my own tin-pot way.'

My mother was clever and went abroad and studied hard and long,
She spoke German fluently, played the piano and sang us many a song.
At ninety-two she daily resolved
That the cryptic crossword must be solved.
At ninety-three, when the chair she sat in
Was much in use, she revised her Latin.
At Christmas, surrounded by paper and string,
Sellotape, labels and everything
She'd refuse our help, and quite firmly say,
'No, I'd rather do things in my own tin-pot way.

I can't use a computer, I don't mean to try,
I seldom leave home and I don't want to fly.
'Dear funny old Granny,' my progeny think
As they check on the car and unstop the sink.
'Dear funny old Granny, she's quite out of date,
I'll just rub up the Aga, it's in such a state!'
Don't think I'm not grateful, I love them to stay
And I'm quite desolate when they've all gone away,
But it's cheering to think on the very next day
I can do things again in my own tin-pot way!

Jean Saunders

SEVEN STAGES AND AGES OF MY LIFE

So this is her then
Said my dad
Gazing at my tiny face
A little girl, not a lad.
'Twas he that took me
When I was five
To my first school
It was with pride.
Soon we were into books
Plays on radio were discussed
Thank goodness that's over
Mum said, looking at us.
I worked down the coal pit
With Dad in his stories
Fought at The Somme
With him in his glories.
We shared the same shelter
When World War Two had begun
A child now eleven
Dangers we learnt to turn into fun.
The time came for marriage
Too young though it seems
My four children I loved
Yet I lost all my dreams.
Now I am older, wiser? Oh no
I live again things now past
More mistakes would I make
It's called, learning slowly, not fast.

Elizabeth Cowley-Guscott

THE FIRST KISS

Their eyes lock across a smoke-filled room,
Smiles are exchanged as she moves closer;
Conversation ensues in earnest.

Both bodies talk of their attraction
As tactile contact increases the stakes;
Strong emotions float to the surface.

Closer they move towards each other,
Pheromones are now thick in the air;
Instinct now guides them to their first kiss.

Gavin Watkins

LIFE IN STAGES

We are all conceived
Within the womb
Through sexual behaviour,
Born to be . . . boy, or girl,

As an infant we grow
To be an adult,
Choosing our own paths,
Of which to follow, to its end

Our own families, we acquire
To love, and to cherish
Just like our, parents did,
In our hours of need

When life, is completed;
Our bodies withered too,
We lay down, our tired figures,
Only to say, farewell

To this wonderful world,
That we grow so accustomed to,
Leaving behind, a very special message,
I love you all so dearly

S J Davidson

SURELY, IT'S SIGNS FROM HEAVEN

The larks they are a singing
Bringing forth a lovely dawn
Breathing life to the flora
Surely it's signs from heaven

Foals frolic along the lea
Hooves swishing - life is free
The birds now seek out a mate
Surely, it's signs from heaven

In every year is mirrored too
The growing grass and the dew
Squirrel stirs with lots to do
Surely, it's signs from heaven

Birds on wing are now soaring
Above the bright blue skies
Leverets they are scurrying
Surely, it's signs from heaven

Almost every day, I gaze about
I sometimes sit and wonder
Is God really pleased with us
Surely, it's signs from heaven.

Robert Jennings-McCormick

MASTICATORY ARCHAEOLOGY

'No eighth,' he said. 'The seventh's badly chipped,
And pocked with caries. Note, the sixth is crowned.
The fifth has gone, its roots untimely ripped
And that amalgam is, I fear, unsound!'
There may be humbler moments when a man
May, supine, wrestle with an inner strife,
Acknowledging omnipotence, who can
But peer, and castigate his dental life.
For no amount of superficial care,
No furtive pick nor brush, dislodging plaque,
Can camouflage raw evidence laid bare
Of old neglect . . .! Dread Sir! no kind remark
Allays my fear that from these aching gums,
True insight of my chewed-up lifestyle comes.

J H Burman

THE THREAD OF LIFE

Cocooned in my cold, black, hollow
Embracing the light-fleeing nothingness,
I await the thread of life.
Plash!
Weightless I spiral below into cavernous depths,
Silky coral depths
Silent ageless depths,
Enrobed with feminine light
Therein to throw.
Liquid body, silvery slow,
Limbs alive, taut,
Diaphanous, I glow.

Deirdre MacLaughlin

THE LONGEST DAY

Large and small
they have to wait
it's the longest day
they cannot get away.

A nurse lends an ear
her smile not so clear
it's the longest day
and they cannot get away.

A cup of tea would be nice
A piece of cake, just one slice
It's the longest day
And they cannot get away.

Come sit with me my friend
a few hours to spend
for it's the longest day
and we cannot get away.

A distant siren shrieks
an ambulance man speaks
it's the longest day
They have to get away.

At last the doctor nods his head
all our fears have sped
it has been the longest day
at last we can get away.

Joan Hands

BYGONE DAYS

What memories these truly are:-
Walks through open and wild countryside.
Watch the shadows of clouds racing one-another
Up hill and down dale,
And see the grass bend in the gentle breeze
See up above the white puffy clouds -
Seemingly suspended upon nothing in a
Lovely blue sky.

Walks through the woodlands where the flowers grow.
See in the woodland glens - the beauty of bluebells
And violets.
We refrain from picking such flowers for that would
Spoil such beauty forever.

We climb up a tree and from the tops we see
A wonderful view of waving treetops, all of different
Shades of green, another world indeed.
And from one's own treetop, and in the sunshine,
We plan our life-span away - by this and that.

But only Jehovah's paradise will solve such plans and wishes,
Then only the above memories will be then fulfilled.
Not just for time alone,
But for eternity.

Norman Mason

CROWDED SPACES, CLOUDED FACES

Regally she glides,
sophisticated - yes;
and so serene;
but sorrow lies
beneath her breast
serenity a screen

There is no peace
no rest, no joy
nor wonderment
just pain and tears
flow from her life
and all of love is spent.

She glides past windows
big boys' toys
fashion, frills and food
her face rejects
her eyes are wet
all of her life dead wood.

How will she know?
How can she know?
My eyes like hers just glisten
not what I know,
but who, and why,
and then she might just listen.

But now she's gone,
her sorrow's left
and I alone and crying;
My hand outstretched
amid the scene
of my dear Saviour dying.

Dennis Studd

BLOODLINE

The border
is drawn
with blood
and with brawn

The treaty
is meaty
and salted
with scorn
and black peppered corpses
still to be born

Still further blood
and still farther borders
shall be drawn
in the dawn of a brand new era.

Gary Austin

LETTERS

Paper chasing thoughts,
loneliness, love declarations,
yesterday's memories.

Reliving time
understanding words
values of the moment.

Today's reality
torn strip by strip
painfully.

Freeing a heart
imprisoned
by word and deed.

Les Merton

JAMIE

My canary is called Jamie
he likes to fly about
I always leave my radio on
whenever I go out

He likes to walk across the floor
he is like a little chicken
If anything happened to Jamie
I would be absolutely stricken

He is a little darling
but when he starts his singing
I am running to the telephone
because I think it's ringing.

Keena Whyte

OUT-OF-BOUNDS
(Based on an abandond Wiltshire village)

It is out-of-bounds now and closed to our sight,
A village shut off, a dead place without life,
A throbbing heart stilled as it gave up the fight.

High on the ridgeway men once toiled with might,
A thriving community, theirs to abide,
It is out-of-bounds now and closed to our sight.

It once had a chapel and school clean and bright,
With cottages, orchards in lush countryside,
A throbbing heart stilled as it gave up the fight.

Men worked on the land, their harvest fields white,
And happy the children, brought up in their pride,
It is out-of-bounds now and closed to our sight.

But when came disaster which caused a great fright,
'Repeal of the Corn Laws' they heard and they cried,
A throbbing heart stilled as it gave up the fight.

From corn crops to pasture, the switch was a slight
Needing only a shepherd, men set aside,
It is out-of-bounds now and closed to our sight,
A throbbing heart stilled as it gave up the fight.

Reg James

WE GOT THERE JUST IN TIME

We got there just in time
To see him get 'Best Actor' -
For his part in *The Great White Bear.*
I remembered we all cheered
So loudly above the rest
The people from the next ten
Or so tables turned to give us 'that look'.

We didn't care much 'cos he'd won.

When I got to the podium
And turned to see they had just arrived
It made my night.
I'd felt stupid sitting at a table,
That was set for eight,
All night on my own.

Gary Lightbody

PEACE IN MY GARDEN

Weeding my garden
Begging my pardon
Alone I wish to dwell
Because I can live it so well
The peace in the mind
The soul comes out kind
Not a word or thought
To make me distraught
Those birds fly by
I don't need to say 'Hi'
Comfort in silence
I don't need all the violence
The way of the world
Does make me curl
So many expectations
From all those damnations
Right here in my garden
I have found my salvation.

Suzan Gumush

I'm Going Off Meat

I'm going off meat altogether
E Coli, Scrapies, Mad Cow.
Could we all live without it, I wonder,
Millions manage to do so somehow.
The country's meat mad so it seems
Safely sheltered from slaughterhouse screams
From blood and from guts
From stink and from fear
All nicely packaged and we don't want to hear.
How it came to our plate
What it is that we eat.
Just buy it and cook it
And shut up and eat.

Jim Scott

WHEN SLEEP EVADES MY NIGHT

What fantasies fill my head
As I lie here in my bed
Of youthful years
Of toil and tears
Things I could have changed - instead

I roam through teenage years
And laugh - I had no fears
The gentleman's date?
Should I be late?
Will this - and others - end in tears

I lie in my bed - of reality
Honeymoon night - gold ring - my speciality
My groom - by my side
I've been - blushing bride
It hadn't just been triviality

Once more I'm alone in my bed
With a lot of memories - it must be said
I've taken the rough and many a tumble
Now I'm beginning to crack and crumble
But I'll carry on life - till I'm dead.

Edna A M Cattermole

EVENING TOUR

You are the man who melts, into
A landscape, or town. Changes with
Summer evenings, walks by sea
Throws stones and shells on a beach
At holidaymakers, keeps children out of reach.
Alarm bells go off around, but admiring glances
Remain at last with the most solid and permanent.
Like the chameleon camouflaged in its cage-stripes,
Dots, and colours are all the rage.
You touch cool water when you feel the bowl.
Like wind, and dust, and smoke you go.
You are the man who dissolves in air -
Slow as grease lightning everywhere.

David Hazlett

INTERLUDE IN LIFE

As I lay down upon the lawn,
My eyes did Heavenwards gaze;
There I saw skies so clear and blue.
High, in the air, a seagull too.
Twigs on the trees, a-hailing life,
Then light green shoots did meet my eyes;
A bee buzzes closer now and then
On dandelion to alight - and -
All was bright and calm around,
Whilst I was lying on the ground.

The Zumac trees did reach so much
Trying to touch the Higher Realms.
The little birds thereon did cluck;
Some did twitter 'mongst the elms.
All kinds of colours, shimmering sheen
To brighten up this garden scene.
Blues, yellows, pinks and white aglow
Gives light to small spruce way below
Near the wall in rustic colours
The meeting place for many lovers.

Pearl Mansell

THE IRS

I hate the Inland Revenue
They've taken all my money
With all the dosh they've had off me
I could be somewhere sunny

Oh, I hate the Inland Revenue
All together now
Why do they look upon my funds
As some sort of fatted cow?

I hate the Inland Revenue
They've got no sense of fun
One minute late in paying them
They threaten with a gun

I hate the Inland Revenue
They're even worse than banks
They'll bleed you dry repeatedly
But never give their thanks

I hate the Inland Revenue
They've off-loaded many tasks
This Self-Assessment thing's a joke
They are robbers without masks

I hate the Inland Revenue
They want everything their way
Next year perhaps I'll call their bluff
And just refuse to pay

Anne Polhill Walton

TOO LATE

How tired we become of life's repetition.
Duties so mundane, we never even ask,
If pleasure's the same,
Or just another mask.

How much better, to have thought
Before we spoke that 'unkind' word,
Or sometimes more, wish we hadn't
Spoken as we had.

How simple waiting for tomorrow:
Can we really take that chance?
If we did, and there just isn't
Would we not be sad?

How often is our wish, we didn't have to bother
With just the smallest task.
How glad we are 'tomorrow'
Without waiting to be asked.

J M H Barton

KITSU

I miss my cat.
She died at sixteen.
Kitsu means little one in Lap.
A friend brought her from
a run down hotel in the East End.
She was sophisticated and a real lady.
Now there is only me.
After the first set of kittens
the vet said that she was
expecting a second.
Eleven balls of fluff slept in the
large grand piano.
The kittens were given away to pupils.
No one returned for piano lessons.

Tom Clarke

I WILL FIGHT ON

I have been fighting a long time
For those rights,
And I do not intend to give up now,
As you will not intimidate my mind,
Because I intend to fight on to the very end,
Until I get what I want.

I will resist with a strong heart,
And I will be as strong as a bull,
That never fails,
And as solid as steel,
That never bends,
Until I win your thoughts.

I will be as hard as a rock,
That never cracks.
My mind will flow as a river,
That never stops.
And I will be as large as an ocean,
That never dries.

I will travel on a wide road,
That never ends.
And I will be around for a long time,
In the end I will intimidate you,
And I promise to win.

Jonathan A Sande

WHEN I GROW UP ...

When I grow up
I'm going to be,
A shopkeeper, a dancer,
That'll be me.
A policeman or fireman
Maybe one of those,
A nurse or a teacher,
A designer of clothes.
A housekeeper or gardener,
Or maybe a maid,
A builder or chauffeur,
I might be involved with trade.
A vet maybe or a star,
But, I think as I slip on my shoes
So many jobs,
Which one shall I choose?

Rachel Gibbins

I WILL NEVER LET YOU GO

As I stood by your side and watched you lay,
Your heart went to sleep and your soul was took away.
No words could have described how I felt inside,
All the love, loss and anger I could not hide.

All our memories I will always treasure,
The short time we spent together nothing could measure.

If I ever had a problem I only had to say,
I'd be sure you were by my side to show me the right way.
The laughs we had and the memories that we made
are in my mind always where they will never fade.

I know I will see you again someday,
In my dreams or heaven there is a way,
You were a great friend and I miss you so,
You are now in my heart and I'll never let you go.

Kelly Marie Crowson (14)

FLOWERS

They continue to come back year after year
An encouraging touch of nature's broom
And the flowers now all reappear
Where were you during winter
Did the swallows take you away
So good of them to bring you back
To make bright the ground so dull and black
Your all more than welcome to stay
My eyes dance over you all so bright
As I try to gather my thoughts
But there's nothing inside me to write
So I'll admire you all I can
And hope you're here when I return
When the world is grand
And you grow through the land
I've no cause for any concern
Who sent out the invitations to play
As they gather nearby the cornfields
The animals are all there today
Mice, hedgehog, vole and squirrel
With a 'how do you do' and a song
Everywhere buzzing with sunshine
All of it natural and so fine
As I lay back to what's going on
Everything nestles comfortably in place
The world would manage somehow I'm sure
With or without the human race
As people take themselves serious
The animal kingdom marches along
The flowers push through
Something old, something new
To mean no one no tears or wrong

Rodger Moir

BLACKSMITH

Iron hard, the blacksmith's muscles glowed,
As copious sweat, from his body flowed.
Bell clear rang anvil now, to hammer's blows
As timeless labour's honest effort flows.

Ox-like strength bends the steels together,
Or, rock-solid, steady, controlling horse's tether,
Yet feather-light can be the blacksmith's hand,
To comfort frightened horse, he strokes with magic wand.

Night's deathly silence, now sit o'er idle forge,
As blacksmith, from huge platter, takes deserv-ed gorge.
No foxy slyness, or deceit, in this man found,
To log-like sleep he falls. His innocence profound.

Howden Brook

DATES

I love the sweet Moroccan dates
    our Christmas season sees,
And succulent Tunisian dates never
              cease to please,
Californian dates just leave me cold,
Though grown 'neath the same sun,
I've pondered what the difference is,
        must be the camel dung.

Barbara Pearton

TO THE DOG

They live to love and serve mankind,
They have no need for sloth
and greed and so
their purpose is decreed.
Such faithfulness will never
leave,
their master's side
until death shall break
the tie,
or age assuage
that lovely key,
The boon of all humanity.

David Bray

A RONDEAU RHYME

Please read this poem, just trying my best,
   I tried so hard at your behest,
to write these words in Rondeau form,
   I will be sad, ay, and forlorn,

If no heed you take of efforts here,
   I have written these words concise and clear
to instil in you poetic cheer,
   by trying to write in iambic verse.
Please read this poem, still trying my best.

No words I write can match the thrill
   of knowing your eyes are reading them still,
what do you think of these poor lines?
   Writing poetry, and keeping up with the times.
Needing to know if my poem is good,
   Please read this poem, still trying my best.

Colin Spicer

SPECIAL TRIBUTE TO PRINCESS DIANA

I shall never forget that sad Sunday when I saw on the news
                                    Princess Diana had died
I could not believe this was true, I couldn't believe my eyes
But the news got worse when they said two more men had died.
Soon the news was spread quickly all over the world so wide
I watched all day to see what caused Diana to die
It was a terrible car crash, when I saw it I wanted to cry.
To think such a beautiful princess should have such a tragic end
She was so affectionate and caring to all the people she did attend
She had a heart of gold and loved everyone
Especially little children and those who were not so young
We do not know what caused the crash so many stories have been told
But there is still a survivor in hospital, so perhaps the truth will unfold.
It's so sad for Prince William and Prince Harry to lose their mum
                                    so young
Princess Diana thought the world of them she idolised her sons
The sadness will grow more and more as time goes by
To lose such a wonderful princess, all over the world, people did cry
Millions of people brought flowers to show how much they cared
Everywhere was covered not a space was spared.
There was a touching scene when the two princes were given flowers
                                    from people there
They shook hands with them and hugged them to show how much
                                    they cared
Prince Charles and Diana's two sisters went to France to bring
                                    Diana home
As they lifted her off the flight it caused a very sad gloom
They took her to St James' Chapel to rest in peace
Till they sorted out the funeral; at the end of the week
It was such a sad day that Saturday, one the world had never seen
Millions of people watching the gun carriage with Diana as it passed
                                    such a memorable scene
My heart was so full as I watched the princes looking so sad
As they walked behind their mum and walking with their dad
That sad day of the funeral we shall always remember
When we watched our lovely princess on the 6th September

All the royal family followed to Westminster Abbey
Even the Queen Mum at her age was there looking very sadly
It was a lovely service the solemn speeches were spoken from
their hearts
Especially her brother Earl Spencer's speech, when he praised his
sister for all her wonderful tasks
Elton John sang a lovely song called, 'Candle in the Wind'
The words were wonderful, the best you would ever find
It has made a record, they are selling millions a day
All over the world in memory of Princess Diana now at peace
she do lay
People have given their condolences in books everywhere
She will make history for years and years and years
They call her the people's princess and Queen of our Hearts
It's so sad she is not with us now and we had to part
I pray God will take care of Prince William and Prince Harry
now they are on their own
May they find happiness and contentment in the future unknown
They took Princess Diana home to where she spent her
childhood days
She is resting on the island there now, she is 'Lady of the Lake'
so they say
But we shall always remember her as our beautiful Princess Diana
now so far apart
But all the loving memories of her we will keep within our hearts.
God Bless you Diana our love for you will never die.

With Love.

Olive Peck

A HAPPY HOLIDAY

Most lads on holiday they expect
lots of sun, sea, sand and sex.
A Swedish 'buty' on the beach
her hair is gold but is it bleach.
To the Spanish girls they are a swine
getting drunk on the local wine.
The German girls they have kissed
as they ski the slope off piste.
Other lads they must fight
to enjoy their great night.
Their holiday is all play
they sleep most of the day.
Their promise to their girlfriends kept
as into a bedroom they crept.
Will this be the same again
just wait till they get off the *plane.*

Colin Allsop

RAINBOWS

Like a multi-coloured banner stretching forth
across the sky.

Curved in a gentle arc that seems so pleasing
to man's eye.

All the colours of Mother Nature are shown for
all to see.

Not in competition, but in perfect harmony.

If man could imitate this wonder, what a marvel
to behold.

Like the colours of the rainbow people living
side by side.

No more racial hatred, no more anguish tears
and pain.

Just a multi-coloured rainbow that gives fresh
hope to man.

Gwyn Thomas

MEMORIES

She sits there waiting patiently
Her friends are coming round
Oh is that them at the door now
She's sure she heard a sound
Her wrinkled face looks eager
She hobbles to the door
But it was just the postman
Two bills upon the floor
She bends down oh so slowly
And shuffles to her chair
She puts the bills behind the clock
She'll not forget them there
She checks her little tea tray
No nothing's been forgot
There's milk and sugar, biscuits too
She's sure she's done the lot
Her little vase of flowers
Looks pretty too, she thinks
They'll enjoy the lovely perfume
Whilst they all have their drinks
She sits there stroking her old cat
The clock begins its chime
Yes any minute they'll appear
Though it's way past the time
They said that they were coming
Perhaps they've been delayed
Well plans can easily go wrong
E'en though they were well laid
Her faded blue eyes close now
In fact she's feeling weary
Oh no I'll have to perk up
Can't have them think I'm dreary

But soon she's nodding in her chair
Excitement made her tired
It also made her forget too
Her friends had long expired.

Jean Smith

PRINCE CHARLES AND HIS LADY

Our Charles has got his lady
To every one's delight,
To see them together
Is a very lovely sight.

To them their love is perfect
And everyone agrees
Like every other couple,
They'll do just as they please.

Their age will make no difference
As she's so very shy
She'll smile and blush so tenderly
As other men go by.

The ring surrounded by diamonds
All set in real gold,
The like of it was never seen,
The like was never sold.

Ruby Brawn

POINTLESS TEARS

When each dawn's greeted with a sigh,
Every single day wishing the end was nigh.
As church bells begin to chime,
You know it's time to say goodbye.
Drive at your destination, unprepared;
Directionless, but remember you never cared.
Murdered each day, with a motive unclear,
Release these pointless fears.
Buy yourself some time in the supermarket of life,
A war zone without a peace accord.
Troops fighting their trouble and strife,
A golf course bunker, with no way out.
Waving your club, you scream and shout.
Tantrums so pointless, to problems set aside;
No energy drink reincarnates a youth that died.
You never miss it 'til its gone they say.
Swimming with friends and sledging in the hay.
Together we followed the trend.
Sniggered through autumn's leaves,
Seasons never seemed to end.
We left the journey, a station too soon,
Left staring at the sunless moon.
Bruised and betrayed, a car without gears;
But hold up your head, wipe away the stain of tears.
A phantom romance, with the girl of your dreams;
A dignity lost or so it seems.
Hard skinned virtues, a cemetery at dusk,
Alone at a bus stop, nobody to trust.
A feverish smile, that has to be tamed;
A portrait picture without a frame,
Look in the mirror, who is to blame?

Martin Watson

PRESSURE

It's pressure, pressure all the time,
God I've got to meet that deadline.
No ifs or buts it's got to be,
On his desk or on my knees.
Begging him for another chance,
To write some silly flowery romance.
I have to write for it's in my blood,
I'd write about heaven if I could.
But I have to write what they do like,
Either that or it's on your bike.
I've got a mortgage and I've got kids,
Believe me I'm not telling fibs.
So I'll just have a heart attack,
Then they'll slot me in the wrack
And get someone else to turn out trash.
Well at least love I gave it a bash.

Don Goodwin

MY IDOL

He walked down a lonely street to Heartbreak Hotel, that man called Elvis who, how lonesome he was, the lonely nights he spent in a dark room. He gave us everything; how they all loved him so, that poor boy from nowhere. There he stood, a lonely man who hurt so much.

He did what he had to do. The songs that he sang for us were rock and gospel too. When you saw him live on stage, you couldn't help but love him. The concerts were all a rage, in every show a wondrous voice when he sang his heart out to you.

The pain he went through no-one knew. His return to sender each time he kissed them with lips that were so tender. His shows are all over now; his rocking hips and gentle ways.

The world rejoiced, it gave him hope and understanding out there. In the dark when you pick up the newspaper there's another expose and the tales grow more bizarre. They were the ones who walked in the wake of a star. It's a crime to treat him this way when he isn't here to defend himself. His fans were always there to see his eyes shine with love.

They just can't help believing that he took drugs to help him sleep and wake. The deep power inside of him made his music fill out hearts with joy. They miss him so. He lived life to the full and did it his way. If you asked him to love you, he would have.

He and his wife went their separate ways when the love they had, had gone. She had suspicions about you, but you never walked out, did you.

He was a prisoner in his own home but his fans never forgot about him. So in love was he when they waited for him, he was all shook up. Do you miss him tonight?

He cried when his mama died and had moods of blue. Can't you see he loved her?

In my mind you haven't gone. When I'm sad I talk to your portrait. I've never felt this way about any other singer as I do about you. When you died I cried, the pain of your loss is life's cost.

You are gone it's true and we weep for you. Our lifestyle dropped when your heartbeat stopped. I close my eyes and think of you and a voice told me you are all right. I was just six years old when I first heard you sing and from that day on it became a lifetime thing.

I had one wish that was to have met you. I am a fool to love you like I do but you made me so happy when I was down and out and gave up on life. I turned to you for help, somehow you gave it too.

When I listen to you and remember that things are not so bad after all, like you Elvis, I went through a pain of loss too when my mother died. You had your ups and downs like all of us do. I don't know what my life would been like without you. Maybe I would have turned to crime and drink too.

My mother is with you now so take good care of her. Now you sit at the right hand of God with her to, in my heart there's a place for you too. I have a memory of blue and lonesome too, losing my mind over you.

Heaven is your final stop and our hearts are broken now. You were the brother I never had and the father that I always wanted. Your wife never ever said that she loved you did she, but it was always on your mind.

You didn't understand why she walked out on you. Now you have gone to a better world where all your brothers and sisters walk hand in hand. When it rained on you it made you happy too. My thanks to you for all the happiness you gave to me and all the other fans to through the years and still do. There will never be another like you, the world is not the same without you.

You walk the golden stairs to your father's house. If you had your life over you would do it all again. The applause has rang out, there is peace in the valley for you after all that. The dream still lives on through the heartache, we the audience were the love of your life.

They stand on stage and copy you but not one of them were as good as you. Now we walk over a bridge filled with troubled waters, don't be cruel teddy bear with long black hair and spending my whole life through loving you and no-one else will do.

Michael Thomas Hill

TIME

It can heal the wounded,
or punish the unloved.
It can make you bitter,
or make you tough.

It makes the survivors,
gives will to the strong.
And crumbles the quitters,
who won't carry on.

But it only makes you,
what you want to be.
A survivor or quitter
give it time - you'll see.

Nicola Raven

QUESTION

What's death like?
I would like to know
Is it a sunbeam that has no glow?
Or it is like a shower of rain
Bringing with it aches and pains . . .

Perhaps it is like a starless sky
or maybe gentle like a sigh?
Usually comes when one is old,
fragile and weak I am told.

So whilst on earth I'll try to live
my life fully, but learn to give
pleasure and help to everyone
so that when my life is done,
I will in heaven rest
because I did my very best.

When I get my curtain call
and have said goodbye to all
friends and family all alike,
the question is,
What's death like?

So when it is my time to go
no-one still will ever know.

Sheila Ryan

MORNING THOUGHTS

Snow has fallen through the night
Nothing moves, no-one in sight
Bushes and trees look so pretty
Fairyland has come to our city
Milkmen and joggers have not yet stirred
Even birds and dogs cannot be heard
Very shortly though the scene will change
Bringing problems to drivers, pedestrians and trains
Cars will get stuck and tempers frayed
Paths will be cleared by many a spade
But none of this will ever affect me
I've nowhere to go and no-one to see
Suddenly I hear a bell
It's time to move from my prison cell.

Barbara Savage

FRIENDSHIP

If you have love
You have life
If you have happiness
You deserve a smile
If you have a heart
You deserve a friend
Someone, whose
Love for you
Is unconditional
Someone, who will
Always be there
To support you
And never, to hurt you
To pick up the pieces
And to hold you
Whether you lose
Or whether you win.

Jacqui Lumb

ALAN TITCHMARSH

Dear Alan,
You had a hard act to follow
When Geoff Hamilton sadly died.
We all miss him so much
So many friends cried.
But now you have taken his place,
With your gentle voice
And with honour and grace.
You always look so happy
In your home at Barley Wood.
You care so much for the wildlife,
As every good gardener should.
Your sense of humour
And your happy smile,
Your ideas and tips
Makes gardening worthwhile.
We sit in our armchairs
On a cold, rainy day
While you chat and work.
We listen to all you say
Stay with us please.
For many, many years
Cheering us with your wit
While busy with your shears.
You also have a strong faith,
It comes across in things you say.
One is close to God in the garden
We find peace and a good place to pray.

Cicely Heathers

DEAR LOVE

Your body worn and tired
Waiting for a call . . . to land's above
Waiting . . . waiting . . . waiting.
The frail hands . . . heavy as lead
Yet warm, soft and tender.
A gentle kiss on forehead placed
A hidden tear . . . I'll miss you dear
But God is waiting . . .
   A special place prepared.
You've loved . . . and been loved
A precious sister you have been
Soon you will be gone to land's above
I'll still love and hold you dear
But wait for me . . .
   I'll see you once more.

Janet Kirkland

KNOWING

Eyes brush eyes and cast a spell,
lips stay silent, but long to tell.
Two minds that do wonder,
two hearts that connect,
the silence is broken but receives no effect.
A passion so strong, a desire too true,
this love was forsaken all because neither knew.

Emma Lewis

My Experiences

I've been there, I've done it, I've tried it all,
my experiences now will be your downfall.
With a lust for life and a lust for love,
I will take what I can and then rise above.
In the past I've been used, to an extent abused,
it's your turn now I will stand accused.

I've weathered it out, I was not always strong,
but stronger than those who won't admit they are wrong.
For those hypocrites the joke will not be on me,
I'll have the last laugh just wait and see.

Forward I'll plunge, there is no turning back,
the confidence I once lost I no longer lack.
Your satisfaction is my one guarantee,
in fact you will wish to come again with me.
But without so much as a glance, I will turn you away,
you took the chance therefore now must pay.

I have weathered it out now inside I am strong,
how can anyone say what I am doing is wrong.
I've maintained the joke will never be on me,
the laugh will be on those who choose not to agree.

My body is yours, every part to explore,
I will take you to heights never reached before.
To the zenith of love, the epitome,
making sure you reach your peak of ecstasy.
You'll long to come back, you will yearn for more,
but once, as I was, you'll be no more than a score.

Yes, I have weathered it out, and am now more than strong,
and perhaps for the most may say I am wrong.
But the joke will never again be on me,
for I've had the last laugh, that's a certainty.

Elsie M Boyle

REPETITION

We eat, we sleep, we walk, we talk, we make money or we just lose.
It's all a repetitive exercise with slight variations we can't choose.
The clouds sail by today but they will also equally sail by tomorrow.
Today is Monday and next week there'll be a Monday, don't sorrow!
Spring, summer, autumn and winter dance by in a tedious roundabout,
Repeat and repeat ad infinitum until your measured time has run out.
So why are you here consuming time which is your precious present?
Everything else is immaterial for your circle has now become
a crescent.
The scurrying years fly, achievements pass by, rags turn into riches.
You think, you drink, your head's sore, your loved one simply bitches.
You brush your teeth, you holiday, you partake in lengthy meetings.
In one year's time, you'll still repeat, just maybe change the seatings.
What is new today is old tomorrow and tomorrow is yesterday's news.
You may or may not accept the luxury of reversing or altering views.
You're anchored on a merciless roundabout subject to pleasure or pain,
Like a blade of grass, sparkling in the sun or heavily beaten by the rain.
Christianity is Shinto is Hindu is Muslim but tells the same tale to you.
It matters very little in the end, for equally, the luxury of time just flew!

T Burke

BIRTH LIFE DEATH

It started when it began
It continued whilst it was going on
It finished when it had ended
And I still live on in spirit

Birth I cannot really remember
Life I think I'd rather forget
Death I do not know all that much about
But it sometimes seems the easy way out

Life can be good if I make it that way
The more grateful I am the longer I'll stay
To deal with each day with all it's troubles and woes
We can all make mistakes but that's the way life goes

Death is when it all comes to an end
I say goodbye to each and every friend
May I be at peace with my soul in heaven's above
Where I experience the gift of everlasting love

Birth Life Death.

Graham Macnab

THE PRICE OF PEACE

Look at mankind
How far has he come
The price of peace
Is a nuclear bomb
Peace for the mighty
War for the poor
Famine drought starvation
Hate and fear and war

Alan Green

RED LIPS, YELLOW HAIR

The moon is red at harvest time, and yellow is the corn.
The men will gather in the corn, the maids will have their fun.
'Oh, shy young man, why do you stand beside the field of grain?'
'The corn must all be gathered in, before there comes the rain.'
He bent his back the live-long day, and toiled beneath the sun.
She promised she would meet him there, when all his work was done.
And soon, beneath the harvest moon, a moon as red as blood,
He wore for her a crown of corn, and poppies still in bud.
She tossed her head, and loosed her hair, as yellow as the corn.
The lips as red as poppies only laughed at him in scorn.
He wound the golden tresses then, so tightly round her neck,
He kept the corn and poppy buds, to wear them in his coat.
The maidens came to find him, by the yellow light of dawn.
They left the young man lying there - a scarecrow in the corn.
The moon is red at harvest time, and yellow as the sun,
The men must gather in the corn - the maids will have their fun.

Brenda Baker

GOOD OLD ENGLAND

My heart belongs to England
With its unpredictable weather.
Good traditional breakfasts,
I'll stay with it forever.
Not for me far off lands,
Sizzling heat or snails.
Food that's unfamiliar,
I'd rather have the dales.

Emmerdale, rolling fields,
A horse with shiny mane.
Good old farmhouse teas,
Forget your sunny Spain.
It's fine for just a holiday,
Maybe now and then.
But give me back my England
once again.

In summer there's the beaches,
Gift shops by the score.
Castles and places of interest,
You couldn't ask for more.
Cosy nights in winter, fires burning bright.
Christmas to look forward
Always a delight!

January's snow we wrap up warm.
Crisp, brisk walks in the country.
Home before the storm.
Blackpool Illuminations,
A splendid sight to see,
Yes - give me good old England
That's the place for me.

Wendy Watkin

THE BLUEBELL WOOD

When springtime comes around again
I think of long ago.
When I rambled through a shady wood
Where bluebells used to grow.
Where sunlight shone through leafy trees
Making dappled shadows on the ground,
With the buzzing of the busy bees,
And bird song all around.
A lonely vixen calling her mate
Startled rabbits scuttling by.
Those trees so tall and majestic seemed
To be reaching for the sky.
But now alas that wood has gone,
In its place a motorway.
No longer we hear sweet nature's sound,
Just traffic day by day.

Ivy Neville

CRESCENT MOON

Would you like to go
and sit on the moon tonight
and cradle on the bottom
and as you swing among the stars
I'll come and sit by you
and hold your hand
Happily we'll swing to and fro'
sitting on the moon
till time to go
Looking at the people
down below
Looking at the moon tonight
and our dream will be over
all too soon
the dream of you and I
together
sitting on the moon.

Connie Moseley

TO A CHAIR

I recall that day we met
Second-hand one Sunday fair
Idle, browsing, unaware
And there she was,
My very mare.

Same old chair
The same, still there
Springs of rust
Moquette threadbare
We are a pair
The worse for wear
Now ancient of a long affair.

John Norcross

NIGHTMARE

News reaches that war is here
Panic, shock, horror, it's all so near
Soldiers games of warfare in the desert heat
Will now be played for real leaving pulses beat
Aching voices swimming the summer's innocence
Slowly ripping away at the stream of resistance
Leaving scattered bullet marks of no return
Shattering loneliness into a land unconcerned
Where plains of twilight dreams lay ruined forever
Lost now in Melancholy's tides of tears
So take back these chains of war, I do not want them as mine
News reaches that war is here.

Saheeda Khan

HE FELT THE PAIN

In those last months
before he died,
he used to sit at the window
and smoke incessantly.

His head was in clouds,
his reflections obscured
and he watched but a fraction
of life pass by each day.

He used to lean forward
to touch the windowpane,
at first scraping, then rubbing
the grimy film away.

He used to hope out loud
his pain would dissolve
but it didn't and no matter
for it meant he was still alive.

And he kept on clinging to life
even when death finally came
and he was surrounded
by his family who finally came,

all claiming to have felt his pain.

Giovanni Malito

THE DAYS OF KELP

Kelp, part of Orkney history
When, from the ebb gathered tang
Kept the strong Lairds in luxury

Poor hardworking cotters by contrary
Collected, dried as kilns sprang
Kelp, part of Orkney history

Burning seaweed reeked, carefree
In the calm island's air did hang
Kept the strong Lairds in luxury

Maybe spoilt crops, irked Nuckelavee
Riots, Peter Fea the leader of the gang
Kelp, part of Orkney history

Year after year continued drudgery
Truant children helped, ignored bell rang
Kept the strong Lairds in luxury

The Kelp boom ended last century
Left Kirkwall mansions built with tang
Kelp, part of Orkney history
Kept the strong Lairds in luxury.

Harrold Herdman

SUN CHAT

How sweetly calls the sun!
No winter gloves or hat
Now winter cold is done.

Who would go seeking fun
To foreign shores at that,
How sweetly calls the sun!

Pull weeds out every one,
Wage war on pest or cat.
Now winter cold is done.

Mowing the lawns begun,
Sun-lounger lying flat,
How sweetly calls the sun!

Barrier cream, sweat run,
Fly swot to deal with gnat,
Now winter cold is done.

Refuge, a shady one!
Though still insisting that
How sweetly calls the sun
Now winter cold is done!

Elsie Norman

THE TREE

Its tall long figure
Towering high above the street
Whispering passers by its tale
Like a sailor back from sea
Sad songs of winter
Looming in the storm
Breaking with a hint of spring
Or with summer warm
And now in its new light
Blooming, dripped in dew
It sings a song of winter's past
And the coming of the new.

Jennifer C Kerr

RED . . .

Red, the colour of a many bloody fights;
The wound made by an ancient blunder buss,
Firing death through its barrel,
Into many an unwary traveller's heart.

Red makes you think,
Makes you think of fear!
Fear? Horrible!
Painful! Unbearable! . . . Fear!

The devil who haunts you all the time,
Who fills your mind with evil,
Red is the colour
The colour of all these things - Red!

Martyn James

WINTER'S FLAME
(For our friend Terry)

Sitting there all alone, his mind,
    numbed almost to bone.
In the flames flitting there,
    pretty pictures beyond compare.
Fathoms deep through burning snow,
    his memories of childhood woes.
When autumn's auburn sunrise glow,
    followed on with silver snow.
Frosty mornings gloomy grey,
    brought on by another day.

Lasting friends in blue and red,
    dangle haunting from the dead.
Ploughing through his fertile field,
    the black of peat revealed.
Frozen earth slumbers deep,
    their voices to keep.
Sleeps the earth till summer frees,
    his golden sun streams.
His misty dreams appear,
    to comfort him throughout the years.

Pamela Naylor

SAY HELLO

She said to say hello
but how was she to know
that time for me
was passing by so slow.
The coffee cup was empty now
and the moon in the sky
was hanging low.
So if you see her passing by
say I love her so.
When she left time
stood still for me
but that was
some time ago.
Now her and I
we shared some time
and I have no regrets.
Now her side of the bed
is always empty
waiting for her return,
so if you see her passing by
this way
say to her I love her so.
Just say to her
I'm still waiting
for her to say hello.

K Lake

VICTORIA FALLS

On the Zambezi River
Victoria Falls.

Deep in to Africa,
The magic roars.

Powerful and strong,
Yet elegant and graceful.
Falling to the river,
From which it has come.

Like its country,
Flowing freely in harmony.

The people of Africa,
Best they forget.

The hatred and racism.

Victoriously destroyed,
By the true beauty of Africa.

The people.

Lee Round

YOU WALKED THE NATURE PATHWAYS

You walked the nature pathways' flourishing fertile ground,
Decorative, sensational, captivating open country all round,
The unblemished bloom of splendour paved with happiness in light,
You gaze unchained and admired astonishing spots a garland of sight,
You loved the freedom and solitude, the fragrance of the air that passed,
Maternal of life that surrounds fruitful, ornamental, bewitching, genuine
a nature world that lasts,

You watched the river flows' torrent sounds of the waters' ways,
You walked on grassland pasture green meadows shining down on you
the sun rays,
You lavished the mountain points to fulfil a deed,
Touching the heavens a crown on each top that you need,
Speechless of breath engulf at the sights,
You were my father, you embraced the heavenly heights.

P M Weaver

A MALVERN VIEW

I cannot be in Malvern without turning to thoughts of you,
Person and place inextricably entwined.
Stepping on wooden bridge, looking eastwards to the view,
Across the Severn Plain to Bredon Hill
Wishing you were here sharing the scene, facing the sun
Together, blessed by the breeze anew.

Gazing long at distant hills forever imprinted on my heart
Where the west wind whispers within.
Hillside homes clustered by the Wyche illumined at day's start,
Several shy skylarks sweep overhead.
Lower slopes thickly wooded, grass golden towards the summit,
I vow from Malvern Hills I'll never part.

Enraptured by what eyes saw, I felt that tingling sensation,
Lost in the wondrousness of it all,
Thinking of you and all we had spoken on that first occasion,
Then tears falling into the stream
Carried I knew not where, except, I hoped, perhaps to you
Containing a message of consolation.

Walking along those best loved paths towards St Anne's Well
Remembered our last conversation,
That you would contact me on our return to walk in the dell,
Of our meeting on this same path
By the pines with branches trailing like a young girl's dress,
I imagined what hearts would tell.

In this place that so stirs the senses, how would we greet?
Even more exquisite to be alone
Merging with the landscape where our two paths might meet
In nature's presence, away from eyes,
Lost in that spellbinding moment, when time at a standstill,
In oneness, and side by side our feet.

Betty Mealand

WARM-HEARTED STAR SUPREME

With fullness of heart I bow my head
As my heart is bathed, immersed.
In radiance that comes from you
And my darkness is dispersed.

Distinguished star with alluring light
Through the clouds your love reveal,
As I look up once more with joy
And my beating heart's appeal.

For a moment rest your light of love
On your journey and impart.
To take the time to smile on me
And my captivated heart.

Many distant stars are bright but cold
And they swiftly pass me by.
Without a smile! Without a sound!
And no thought for glaze of eye.

With fullness of heart I reach to touch
Bright warm-hearted star your beam.
For Cilla dear, you shall remain,
A warm-hearted star supreme!

Peter James O'Rourke

OUR GOOD NEIGHBOURS

We've got such friendly neighbours,
    Who help us all they can.
They give their leisure time to make
    Our garden spick and span.
They're such good and caring neighbours -
    Volunteer to tend and toil;
Down on their knees to graft and weed -
    And dig our hard clay soil.
Our grand and helpful neighbours know
    We're getting on in years.
They mow the lawn and plant the bulbs -
    Even sharpen up our shears!
We're so grateful to these neighbours -
    To repay them is our aim;
But when we offer pay they just
    Refuse it once again.
We're blessed with such kind neighbours,
    To please they always try
To sweep away our worries and
    We're glad they live nearby.

Richard Mayor

GULLS IN CONWAY

So I went to Conway
in Wales one day!

I ate sandwiches of chicken
and a gull came a picken!

I ate one round
and then I found!

As I took a bite from the other round
he took it from my mouth and hand, by gum!

The very next day
I went away -

To Llandudno, and do say
I ate the two chicken sandwiches, oh lay!

On the bus let me say
no gulls about. No wait!

But, let me say
I liked to sit by the sea in Conway!

Marie Barker

BOXING

Our brother Tom
No big head
Did not want to carry on
Acting in school plays or in the choir
So instead - later
Took lessons in boxing
In King Edward's building, St Pauls
For the Post Office Sports

Was given gift for being
Telegraph Boy who was the smartest

Would have chosen the Navy
Did not want to upset mum
So waited until 'called up' for the Army

On the ship coming back from the Middle East
The soldiers planned boxing contest
And in looking for someone
A mate from the Post Office suggested Tom

Mum would have had a fit I'd say
His rival was much older anyway

They thought Tom was terrific
By the time we knew
Tom had his medal

All he ever said later was

'Boxing is fighting now
No longer *scientific.*'

Phyllis O'Connell (Hampson)

NATURE'S DEVOTION

Mother Nature, she was wise,
Made vegetarian 'green', to ease our eyes.
Those flowers, their blossoms, of many hues,
Yellow, pink, white, red and blues.
Their scents will drift everywhere,
Releasing perfume to sweeten our air.
Without moisture all would die,
She sends the rain from the sky.
Without her sun and her rain
No vegetation, or I, would live again.

Brian Marshall

THE PEACE OF YESTERDAY

Oh how I long for yesterday
When the world seemed safe and sane
When outside children all day could play
And come safely home again
Where contentment lay in simple things
And our own entertainment we made
With tops and whips and rope skipping
And for running errands pocket money were paid
No holidays abroad or expensive trainers
But our hours spent at home were all enjoyed
We didn't hear many complainers
And most of our dads were employed
They say the best things in life are free
Make of them the best you can
If you try your best you will surely see
All that's good in your fellow man
Money can't buy happiness or love
It comes from within your heart
Greed, envy and ego we should all give a shove
And sharing, caring and love impart
Oh how I long for yesterday
When I was an innocent child
If only life were like that today
Instead of greedy, vicious and wild.

Doris Davis

BEAUTY

Blow, blow ye summer winds
Kithness seeds do yonder drift
To rest upon the infinite sod
To display its princely gifts

Blow, blow ye summer winds
O'er the oceans vast and deep
Let pure vapours there so rise
To give life for them to reap

Blow, blow ye summer winds
Let the earth blossom in majesty
With aspects of enshrinment
And a fragrance of secrecy

Blow, blow ye summer winds
Murmuring over dales and meadows beyond
Bluebells sway to and fro
Ringing out their silent song

Summer winds again will yield
To the winter's awesome gloom
Sweet darling buds of May doth sleep
Summer to rest all too soon

Once again the land in slumber abides
When winter takes its toll
But will all the love nature gives
Beauty still lies within the soul.

W Beavill

GRANDDAD ALLSOP COME BACK

At the start of World War II
That Lord Haw Haw knew
He was never wrong
He warned the folk of Edmonton.

In Germany so far
They see the Edmonton Elkerzar.
A shelter folk had formed
Hitler wanted it raised to the ground.

In heaven Granddad Allsop did see
And said I want to let it be.
Came back from the grave
His family he must save.

On the landing they heard his sound
Safe to the shelter underground.
With his strong love
With the bombers so soon above.

The bombs they did fall
Put shrapnel in nan's wall.
Thanks to him they were alive
Granddad Allsop see they *survive*.

Colin Allsop

I'm Not In A Muddle I Just Want To Cuddle With You

Well I don't want to miss I think it would be bliss
To spend the whole night through with you
I'm working overtime so I can buy the wine
And bring a carry out home too

Then we could settle down and pass the mints around
And watch the fire burn down low
Sit on the Persian rug where we could kiss and hug
Then I'd tell you I love you so

No need to hesitate we wouldn't want to wait
Until the marriage bans are read
We could forget our cares as we went up the stairs
Where we would cuddle up in bed

Oh what a perfect night, oh what a blissful flight
Of fantasy a dream come true
But I don't dare to speak, my knees are much too weak
For me to make a pass at you.

Michael Shimmin

ON BEHALF OF OUR CLIENT

Dear Mister Klunk, of the ACME Patent
Trading Corporation, We wish to claim
Compensation for our injured client,
Wile E Coyote (Genius) who's aim
In buying your *Mark Five Supa Nova*
Rocket boots was catching himself dinner.
(Wringing the beep-beep neck of that Bovva-
Bird, Speedicus Maximus or Road-Runner,
Was incidental.) Wile E was starving.
Your 'Tell 'im to open a tin of beans'
Remark was insensitive. Inspecting
Your firm's part in his past injuries seems
To call for more money than when your blokes
Sold him that chain saw kite-bike. That's all folks!

Arthur Chappell

ONLY YOU

Time passes by and no matter how hard I try, I can't get you out of my head. This feeling of loss and emptiness sometimes makes me wish I was dead.

As the days go on and the nights seem so long. Looking for one look at your sweet face, but you have disappeared and not left a trace.

In my heart you're always with me and for the rest of eternity this always will be. Thoughts race wildly straight through my mind as without you I am lost as you were my greatest find.

Everyday dreaming of you as it's the only way I know how to get through. Birds flying so high in the sky as I wait for the day to be given one more try.

I walk down the street and I walk through the park. I walk in the light and I walk in the dark. Lost without you to hold me real tight as I am now alone all through the night.

Life is too short to row and fight, give me a chance and I will prove that us both together is so right.

Time still passes by as I wait for you to walk through the door. A click at the keyhole, a light at the door, your shadow shining on the floor. I smile so happily, my face shines with glee and I thank God you have come back to me.

Steven Jackson

WHAT DO WE EXPECT

Just imagine if we knew our future destiny
How dull our life would be
Our happiness laid out for us
No striving or trying
Our life would be a
Mystery no more.

J Campbell Jones

THE PORNO AGE

At first life's simple pleasures; wine, love and song
Three innocent endeavours, things of beauty, amour, mystique and
true love's song
Where did we go wrong? For suddenly, without a tear, porno's here.

'Sodom and Gomorra' knew which way to steer!
The greatest thing since incarnation
The latest commercial innovation

Sex and love are both an entity, it seems
A fact of life, an animal desire to be fulfilled
Human models, before an ever hungry audience, pose gyrating in
erotic passion
Divorced of all their old beliefs, devoid of all their clothes or clad
perchance in bras or briefs or kinky gear, to raise a cheer

Though at first there was a spot of bother from people who thought
that sex should take its natural means
Sex has become a sort of ancient fodder, revitalised on lurid magazines

Or a genital salad, a pervert pudding, meted out in ever-increasing
dosage, as is the want, and with ever increasing profits from life's
most lucrative source, the eternal font!

Is it good or is it bad?
Surely, to encourage and exult infidelity, bisexuality, perverts
and sadism, is absolutely *mad.*

Miles Everidge

INHERITANCE

The vulture will soon come after the death of someone.
Even distant relatives at the reading of the will they will
appear, and very often when the deceased were alive, this
relative never bothered to visit them or be good friends.
But if there is anything to grab, they are the first.
This is happening in our time that sons and daughters never
cared for the mum and dad. But as soon as they are dead,
they run to be present at the funeral and pretend to cry for
the loss of the mother or the father. They think that they
show to the bereaved family that they really are sorry for
the deceased! If they have no respect and care for the
parent when they are alive, they should not claim the
inheritance. The law should be changed for the respect of
all the parents. They make a will or give the deed to a son
or daughter they thought at the time that it was right.
But soon they found out the true fact of life. They have
been thrown out of their own house that they lived all their
life. Some thing must be done to help everyone!

Antonio Martorelli

SUBMISSIONS INVITED
SOMETHING FOR EVERYONE

ANCHOR BOOKS '99 - Any subject,
light-hearted clean fun, nothing unprintable
please.

WOMENSWORDS '99 - Strictly women,
have your say the female way!

STRONGWORDS '99 - Warning!
Age restriction, must be between 16-24,
opinionated and have strong views.
(Not for the faint-hearted)

All poems no longer than 30 lines.
Always welcome! No fee!
Cash Prizes to be won!

Mark your envelope (eg *Poetry Now*) *'99*
Send to:
Forward Press Ltd
1-2 Wainman Road, Woodston,
Peterborough, PE2 7BU

OVER £10,000 POETRY PRIZES
TO BE WON!

Judging will take place in October 1998